THE SELF-DISCOVERY JOURNAL

The Self-Discovery Journal

52 Weeks of Reflection, Inspiration, and Growth

Yana Lechtman, PsyD

ROCKRIDGE
PRESS

For general information on our other products and services or to obtain technical support, please contact our Customer Care Department within the United States at (866) 744-2665, or outside the United States at (510) 253-0500.

Rockridge Press publishes its books in a variety of electronic and print formats. Some content that appears in print may not be available in electronic books, and vice versa.

Interior and Cover Designer: Erin Yeung
Art Producer: Sara Feinstein
Editor: Jed Bickman
Production Editor: Nora Milman
Production Manager: Martin Worthington

Illustration used under license from Creative Market/Marsala Digital. Author photo courtesy of Tzipor Mia.

ISBN: Print 978-1-64876-767-8
R0

This Journal Belongs to

_____

Introduction

Whether you have received this journal as a gift or gifted it to yourself, consider it an invitation to embark on a journey of self-discovery. You may be struggling with challenges, looking for direction, or simply trying to connect to yourself on a deeper level. Whatever the case, this journal will launch you on a path of curious exploration, courageous reflections, and poignant questions. It will require an honest look into different aspects of your life. You may be simultaneously excited and worried about what you will discover; that is quite common. Take that leap of faith in yourself and trust that you can handle whatever comes.

Working as a clinical psychologist in New York City, I was honored to meet many people from different ages and walks of life. That experience prompted me to delve into my own self-discovery. My multicultural background created a need for me to hone my identity, which required a lot of introspection and soul-searching. The practice of self-reflection allowed me to adapt my self-concept, my attitudes, and my behaviors to the contexts of my relationship with myself, with others, and with my environment. Being able to understand myself and the motives behind my attitudes or behaviors gives me the know-how and the tools to respond to life's demands in the most effective ways.

Because change is one of the only constants in our lives, it is important to keep an open and flexible mind. Just as working out physically strengthens your body and makes it more flexible, self-discovery allows your mind to gain strength and flexibility. The practice of self-reflection through journaling will help you question your thoughts, behaviors, and actions to determine whether they are working or there is room for improvement and what that improvement may be. Once you become more reflective and self-aware without judgment or shame, you will find that your life is filled with choices, and you will be able to accept and adjust to change and better tolerate adversity. Remember, this is a practice, so it requires time and effort. Progress is not always linear; challenges are likely to emerge as you allow different parts of yourself to come to light.

Slowing down and looking into yourself takes courage. It is natural to want to avoid unpleasant realities, thoughts, and emotions as a way to protect yourself and others. But rest assured, there is a method to the madness, and you will emerge from the experience with strength and understanding you didn't previously think possible. Over the next 52 weeks, you will be engaging with a series of prompts that build on one another. Each week begins with a quotation. Look at the words of others, take them in, and allow yourself to be inspired. Then approach the prompts as guides to understanding your inner world, your actions, and your genuine desires. Be honest and vulnerable. Try to let go of any expectations you might have for this journal or yourself. Simply allow yourself to be nonjudgmentally curious about what comes up for you as you address each prompt.

I hope that this adventure of self-exploration will help you uncover and discover your most authentic self. I hope you will be able to appreciate all that you are and learn which aspects of yourself you want to let go and which parts you would like to grow.

PART ONE

Self-Awareness

You are a unique being, but in the midst of your busy life and with so much information coming from so many directions, sometimes it is difficult to recognize and express your individuality. If you are not fully aware of what your unique self looks like, you may take the path of least resistance and simply follow the crowd and conform to norms. But this path suppresses your authenticity and may leave you feeling dissatisfied with your life.

Self-awareness is the conscious awareness and knowledge of your own uniqueness. This is exactly what you will work to discover in the first part of this journal. Each week, you will work to uncover a different aspect of yourself: your beliefs, thoughts, and feelings. You will be challenged to take an honest look into yourself and your present, past, and hopes for the future. Each discovery may be something you like about yourself, or it may be something you'd like to work to change. Try to be as honest with yourself as possible, even in the moments when it feels unpleasant. Discomfort in your work of self-discovery helps lead you to true self-awareness and growth.

"If you want to change and grow, then you must know yourself and accept who you are before you can start building."

—JOHN C. MAXWELL

Defining who you are can feel challenging; after all, how do you summarize your whole being in a few words? Try to let your mind run free and think of five adjectives that describe you. Think of examples of behaviors or situations that illustrate each adjective. If you cannot think of an example, replace that adjective with one that might be more representative of who you really are.

I am an energized person. I prefer to almost never live life in cruise control. Whether it is my career, my relationships, or my internal work & self development, I would always like to be experiencing a sense of growth & forward motion. I am a very curious person. I am determined. I am highly organized. I am quite outgoing & sociable.

At times, we all dream of having certain traits or qualities. Imagine that a genie popped out of a bottle and offered to instill in you any five characteristics you desire. What five qualities you would like to have the most, and why?

* Calmness - I so admire people who are still in the face of adversity, but also in moments of normalcy. Individuals who carry themselves with a certain comfortable fluidity.
* ~~Self Reliant~~ Self Reliant: I want to depend on myself alone for joy, comfort, finances, health, and future goals. I know that realistically I want others to be a big part of each of the facets of my life, but having a firm foundation in self reliance first seems & feels imperative
* carefree
* ~~Anxious~~ Free from anxiety
* Content

Look at your five adjectives from the first prompt, and then at the qualities you wished for from the genie in the second prompt. How different are they from one another? What do you believe are the barriers stopping you from acquiring the qualities you want? Are there ways to overcome the barriers?

I believe the first qualities are very fast paced, intense, and forward moving qualities. The second adjectives represent a slow down that allows me to remove some of the self inflicted pressures I often place on myself & my life. I also want to be more independent, and I think there is nothing stoping me from achieving this other than constant, consistent action of self reliance. I want to keep practicing relying on myself more & more every day

WEEK 2

"A child's life is like a piece of paper on which every person leaves a mark."

—CHINESE PROVERB

Our childhood experiences are the building blocks on which we build our adult selves. Consider some of your experiences in your childhood. What can you identify as significant experiences that contributed to the person you are now? Think of both pleasant and unpleasant experiences.

As a child, my parents were divorced. We moved around houses a ton. My sister was anorexic. Instability, unpredictability, fear, shame, embarassment. We had a big, safe home with lots of light. We had a pool & lots of friends over. We had games, toys, & consistent food on the table. Mom was almost always home with us. Safe, fun, consistent, stable, present. We took family trips. We made mother's day break fast. We didnt worry about much. This changed when I was in middle school

We learn to navigate our world through our experiences. We expect the world and people in it to respond to us similarly to what we know from past experiences. Consider the experiences in the previous prompt. Can you identify some ways you carry those experiences with you to this day? For example, you may anticipate that you will experience rejection and disappointment, so you won't reach out for help.

I have a complex relationship with those who show up inconsistently in my life. When people are not dependable, I feel emotionally threatened by the turbulance. When I have a friend who is emotionally scattered & inconsistent, I believe my healthy response should be to take space. I do not need to be critical of them. I can identify how their behaviors are feeling threatening to my inner peace & without drama or confrontation, simply create a boundary that works to maintain a safe distance for my emotional safety. I will tell Cara "the way we communicated about Laguna was challenging for me. I felt like you did not really want me there, which

Our expectations shape our dialogue with the world. Considering your observations about your past experiences and how you carry them with you into your present, are there ways you think or act that might reinforce these patterns? For example, if you anticipate that your request will be denied, you might not express that request in the most effective way—or at all.

hurt my feelings. In the future, even if the plan is loose, it would be helpful to me if you simply communicated the plans looseness so I can still feel included in what is going on. If you only communicate 5 minutes before, it feels like you do not want me there and are not considerate of my needs for communication.

"Rather than being your thoughts and emotions, be the awareness behind them."

—ECKHART TOLLE

We are ever-evolving, yet there is a core to who we are and how we engage with the world. What are some recurrent themes in your thoughts about yourself, the world, or people around you? Are there thoughts you habitually try to push away?

About myself: I am likeable, fun, active, engaging, charismatic. I am not hard working enough, I ruin relationships overtime. I will never meet my life partner bc I ruin relationships. The world is awesome but filled with a 50/50 mixture of good & bad humans. I try to push away the connections & relationships I have with my family members because I generally find them to be painful & sad & emotionally draining. I am going to make more of an effort to spend quality time with my dad

We all have unique relationships with different emotional experiences. Some emotions are more familiar and easier for us to connect to than others. Are there emotions you experience more frequently or express more freely? Are there other emotions you rarely allow yourself to feel?

_____

_____

_____

_____

_____

_____

_____

_____

_____

_____

_____

_____

_____

_____

_____

_____

_____

Look back at your previous answers. Can you recognize how your core thoughts and feelings influence and reinforce one another? Are there specific thoughts and feelings that lead you to suffering? Do you feel sadness, anger, jealousy, disappointment? Or are you wary of feelings of pride or joy? Imagine yourself in a scenario that might lead to experiencing such feelings. Be as specific as you can. Can you identify how avoiding certain thoughts and feelings could influence your life for better and worse? How are they protecting you and/or hindering you?

_____

_____

_____

_____

_____

_____

_____

_____

_____

_____

_____

_____

_____

_____

WEEK 4

"Your vision will become clear only when you can look into your own heart. Who looks outside, dreams; who looks inside, awakes."

—CARL JUNG

Being fully self-aware includes recognizing the people, things, and situations you are grateful for. There are so many benefits to gratitude, like improved self-esteem, better physical health, greater empathy, and more joy. Write down five small things (e.g., a morning cappuccino) and five major things you feel grateful for today.

_____

_____

_____

_____

_____

_____

_____

_____

_____

_____

_____

Bring your gratitude to the surface by expressing it externally. Write a letter to someone you feel grateful for. (You don't have to send it.) Include details about why you are grateful for that person.

_____

_____

_____

_____

_____

_____

_____

_____

_____

_____

_____

_____

_____

_____

_____

_____

_____

_____

_____

Think of ways that you can incorporate gratitude into your daily rituals. How can you make being grateful a habit? For instance, maybe each morning when you brush your teeth, you take a minute to list three things you feel grateful for that day. Or consider saying goodnight to your kids or significant other with a few words of gratitude for them a few times a week.

_____

_____

_____

_____

_____

_____

_____

_____

_____

_____

_____

_____

_____

_____

_____

_____

_____

WEEK 5

"Argue for your limitations, and sure enough, they're yours."

—RICHARD BACH

Many times, we fuse our feelings and thoughts with reality: A fear or thought that we do not excel at something leads us to believe that we are really not good at it. Maybe we haven't even tried it. Consider your recurrent thoughts and feelings; are there some thoughts that you have accepted as fact without ever really testing them?

_____

_____

_____

_____

_____

_____

_____

_____

_____

_____

_____

_____

Reflect on the ways you might be reinforcing and acting upon your limiting beliefs about yourself. Can you unearth any fears or concerns about what might happen if you let go of these beliefs?

_____

_____

_____

_____

_____

_____

_____

_____

_____

_____

_____

_____

_____

_____

_____

_____

_____

_____

How can you reinforce positive thoughts and change your limiting thoughts to be more empowering? For example, "Although I am not experienced in X, I can always practice it and get better." How do you imagine these new thoughts would influence your life?

_____

_____

_____

_____

_____

_____

_____

_____

_____

_____

_____

_____

_____

_____

_____

_____

_____

_____

WEEK 6

"Self-awareness is the ability to take an honest look at your life without any attachment to it being right or wrong, good or bad."

—DEBBIE FORD

Everyone has things they are naturally better at. Knowing your strengths and weaknesses can help you navigate situations in life more effectively and peacefully. Think of a family member, a good friend, your boss, and another person who is meaningful to you. What do you imagine each of them would identify as some of your strengths and your weaknesses?

_____

_____

_____

_____

_____

_____

_____

_____

_____

_____

_____

Imagine you had no weaknesses or limitations. What would you be able to do? (We're not talking superpowers here!) Are there any new hobbies or habits you would develop?

_____

_____

_____

_____

_____

_____

_____

_____

_____

_____

_____

_____

_____

_____

_____

_____

_____

_____

_____

Considering your response to the previous prompts, are there ways you can enlist your current strengths to overcome some of your weaknesses and develop new strengths you aspire to have? Which weakness would you start with?

_____

_____

_____

_____

_____

_____

_____

_____

_____

_____

_____

_____

_____

_____

_____

_____

_____

_____

_____

"**Fight your fears and you'll be in battle forever, face your fears and you'll be free forever.**"

—LUCAS JONKMAN

No one is shielded from having fears and anxieties. Some people are afraid of mice or being wrong and ridiculed, while others are afraid of the unfamiliar feelings of being loved or successful. Try to take an honest look into yourself: What causes anxiety for you? Are there fears that make you want to move away from an object or experience or leave you paralyzed in its presence?

_____

_____

_____

_____

_____

_____

_____

_____

_____

_____

_____

_____

Understanding your fears may help you soften them. Think of one of your fears. Do you have any ideas about how it came to be a fear? Did you have a personal challenging experience? Or maybe you learned this from a loved one who instilled this fear in you. Try to identify if there might be any barriers to letting go of the fear. For instance, can you imagine any unfavorable consequences to your not having the fear anymore?

_____

_____

_____

_____

_____

_____

_____

_____

_____

_____

_____

_____

_____

_____

_____

_____

_____

Fears develop as a way to protect oneself, but the experience of facing any fear is empowering. Success allows us to continue conquering more and more fears. Is there any fear, even a small one, that you are willing to face? What are the actual steps you would take to expose yourself to that fear? Suppose you are afraid of dogs; you can start facing this fear by looking at puppies at a pet shelter through the glass or going on a walk with a friend's dog and petting it.

_____

_____

_____

_____

_____

_____

_____

_____

_____

_____

WEEK 8

"When you replace judgment with curiosity, everything changes."

—ROBYN CONLEY DOWNS

Think of your perception of others. Sit on a bench and people watch for a few minutes to see what you notice about others. Think of some of your family members, your friends, and random people. What are the most frequent thoughts that come to your mind? Are there any common themes?

_____

_____

_____

_____

_____

_____

_____

_____

_____

_____

_____

_____

We all make judgments about others; it is the natural way of our minds. Consider your answer to the previous question. Can you decipher which of those thoughts are objective observations (e.g., many people have dark hair) and which are your own judgments (e.g., people with dark hair are much more beautiful)? Can you observe other judgments you tend to have?

_____

_____

_____

_____

_____

_____

_____

_____

_____

_____

_____

_____

_____

_____

_____

_____

_____

Judgments are like a reflex, an unconscious way our minds make sense of the world around us. As your self-awareness to your own judgments grows, it can help you act in more conscious ways, giving you the choice of how to respond to people and situations as opposed to following your "judgment reflex." Are there judgments that are important for you to keep? For example, you might judge those who volunteer at animal shelters as generous people and want to associate with them. Are there other judgments that interfere with your life to the point that you would like to let them go?

_____

_____

_____

_____

_____

_____

_____

_____

_____

_____

_____

_____

_____

_____

WEEK 9

**"Self-consciousness is a disease.
Self-awareness is health."**

—OSHO

Our judgments are not just pointed toward others. We tend to
be harsh critics of ourselves and to think everyone else judges
us similarly. What aspects of your own appearance, behavior,
and personality do you tend to be self-conscious about?

_____

_____

_____

_____

_____

_____

_____

_____

_____

_____

_____

_____

Under what circumstances are your self-conscious thoughts more present (e.g., with certain people, areas of life, or internal states)? What feelings do they bring up? Do these thoughts and feelings make you act differently? Be as specific as you can.

_____

_____

_____

_____

_____

_____

_____

_____

_____

_____

_____

_____

_____

_____

_____

_____

_____

Think of a friend who might experience similar self-conscious thoughts. What do you think you might tell that friend who shared those thoughts with you? Is there a way for you to be kinder and more compassionate toward yourself when self-conscious thoughts come to your mind? Write an understanding dialogue with yourself.

_____

_____

_____

_____

_____

_____

_____

_____

_____

_____

_____

_____

_____

_____

_____

_____

_____

_____

WEEK 10

"Being self-aware is not the absence of mistakes, but the ability to learn and correct them."

—DANIEL CHIDIAC

Mistakes, failures, and disappointments are natural and inevitable parts of life. Reflect on your experiences and note what you consider to be mistakes and failures in your life and what makes them that. Be specific.

_____

_____

_____

_____

_____

_____

_____

_____

_____

_____

_____

_____

_____

Mistakes and failures, though they can be painful, are also opportunities to learn, improve, and even open unexpected doors. Reflecting on your experiences in the previous question, what were the positive aspects to your failures? Were there any small successes you could detect amid the failure?

_____

_____

_____

_____

_____

_____

_____

_____

_____

_____

_____

_____

_____

_____

_____

_____

_____

Reflect on your broader perspective about failure and success. How is each defined, and by whom? In your worldview, are you attuned to successes in life or mostly to failures? How much do imperfections color your judgment of and experience with success?

_____

_____

_____

_____

_____

_____

_____

_____

_____

_____

_____

_____

_____

_____

_____

_____

_____

WEEK 11

"True belonging doesn't require you to change who you are; it requires you to be who you are."

—BRENÉ BROWN

Belonging is an innate need of humans. Although each of us feels this need to different degrees, being part of a group—whether it be our family or a bigger community—is imperative. Reflect and identify how your need for belonging looks. Under what circumstances do you feel fully accepted?

_____

_____

_____

_____

_____

_____

_____

_____

_____

_____

_____

_____

At times, belonging does not come easily. How does it influence your thoughts and behaviors when that need is not met? Try to think about what you do in those moments: Do you tend to attempt to fit in at the expense of your true self? How does that, in turn, affect your feeling of belonging? Your feelings about yourself?

_____

_____

_____

_____

_____

_____

_____

_____

_____

_____

_____

_____

_____

_____

_____

_____

_____

_____

Reflecting on the previous questions, try to identify which core aspects of yourself, when accepted by others, make you feel as though you belong. Which aspects of yourself, if changed to fit in with others, would feel inauthentic to you?

_____

_____

_____

_____

_____

_____

_____

_____

_____

_____

_____

_____

_____

_____

_____

_____

_____

_____

WEEK 12

"We are addicted to being the way we are."

—DON MIGUEL RUIZ

We all have an internal narrative about who we are and an idea of how we should or ought to be. Looking back at previous weeks' entries in this journal, what is your elevator pitch about yourself? Try to sift it down to the essence of you—your most cardinal being.

_____

_____

_____

_____

_____

_____

_____

_____

_____

_____

_____

_____

_____

_____

_____

We are continuously changing, even if we are not fully aware of the process. Were there things you discovered about yourself in past weeks that did not fully match your current perception of yourself? Maybe you realized you are less optimistic than you thought, or maybe there is a fear you didn't fully overcome yet.

_____

_____

_____

_____

_____

_____

_____

_____

_____

_____

_____

_____

_____

_____

_____

_____

_____

We are changing with each experience, but we tend to strongly hold on to our internal stories and beliefs about who we are. Are you willing to embrace what you discovered in the first prompt and let go of those beliefs you noted in the second? What could stand in your way to accepting the person you truly are, and how could you overcome it?

_____

_____

_____

_____

_____

_____

_____

_____

_____

_____

_____

_____

_____

_____

_____

_____

_____

WEEK 13

"Find out who you are, and do it on purpose."

—DOLLY PARTON

Look at what you have discovered in the past three months.
Reflecting on the aspects of yourself that you have become
more aware of during the past weeks, are there parts of
your self-perception that you think you will find harder to
readjust? Maybe it is unfamiliar to be seen as successful or
fearful. What would it mean to you to accept these aspects
of yourself?

_____

_____

_____

_____

_____

_____

_____

_____

_____

_____

_____

Can you draft a contract with yourself that lists the overall commitments that you want to make to yourself in terms of adding and enhancing qualities and thereby developing new habits and behaviors in your life?

_____

_____

_____

_____

_____

_____

_____

_____

_____

_____

_____

_____

_____

_____

_____

_____

_____

_____

_____

Write down the ways you can make at least three of those commitments a reality. Be as specific and practical as possible, and write all the steps you will need to take to make these happen.

_____

_____

_____

_____

_____

_____

_____

_____

_____

_____

_____

_____

_____

_____

_____

_____

_____

_____

PART TWO

Values

Values are the principles that guide our lives, belief systems, and behaviors. Whether you are fully aware of your values or you are not conscious of what they are, your core values dictate how you navigate different situations in life.

In this section, you will develop an awareness of the values you live by, reflect on which values are most profoundly important to you, and uncover any values that may be hindering you. You will also discover practical ways to live by your values so that you can continue walking on the path that feels most authentic to who you are.

WEEK 14

"**Your values are embedded within you irrespective of whether you discover them or not. Even if you never find them, they still govern your life.**"

—DR. PREM JAGYASI

Take a moment to reflect on what is truly important to you in your life. What makes you excited, passionate, energetic, anxious, sad, and fearful? Make sure to think of all aspects of your life: social, family, romantic, professional, community, spiritual, and physical.

_____

_____

_____

_____

_____

_____

_____

_____

_____

_____

_____

Looking at the previous prompt, consider how to group these important aspects of real life into buckets that represent different values. Feel free to add or remove values while you are exploring your relationship with each.

Now go over the buckets of values you created, and identify 10 to 15 values that feel the most important and authentic to you.

_____

_____

_____

_____

_____

_____

_____

_____

_____

_____

_____

_____

_____

_____

_____

_____

_____

"There's no need to be perfect to inspire others. Let people get inspired by how you deal with your imperfections."

—ZIAD K. ABDELNOUR

Think of a few people who inspire you. What values of theirs would you like to embrace? Make sure to think of all aspects of life: social, family, romantic, professional, community, spiritual, and physical.

_____

_____

_____

_____

_____

_____

_____

_____

_____

_____

_____

_____

_____

_____

Now think of a few people who you do not respect. What is it about them that irks you? What values of yours do they violate? Again, make sure to think about all aspects of your life.

_____

_____

_____

_____

_____

_____

_____

_____

_____

_____

_____

_____

_____

_____

_____

_____

_____

_____

_____

Now look at values you noted in the two previous questions. Do they match the values you have listed as most important to you last week? Are there values you would like to add to or remove from the earlier list?

_____

_____

_____

_____

_____

_____

_____

_____

_____

_____

_____

_____

_____

_____

_____

_____

_____

WEEK 16

"Values are like fingerprints, nobody's are the same, but you leave them all over everything you do."

—ELVIS PRESLEY

Look at the list of values you have created and grouped in the previous weeks. Consider which values are more important to you personally and rank them in order.

_____

_____

_____

_____

_____

_____

_____

_____

_____

_____

_____

_____

_____

Think about your most important values. Are those truly important to you personally, or do they reflect societal or familial expectations? Consider the values you learned from your family, friends, and society. Which values actually resonate with your true self? Are there any that you would like to let go of? Or reinforce?

Reflecting on all the values you identified as the most important to YOU, choose your five core values.

_____

_____

_____

_____

_____

_____

_____

_____

_____

_____

_____

_____

_____

_____

_____

_____

_____

_____

_____

_____

WEEK 17

"Keep your thoughts positive, because your thoughts become your words. Keep your words positive because your words become your behavior. Keep your habits positive because your habits become your values. Keep your values positive because your values become your destiny."

—MAHATMA GANDHI

Think about the five core values you identified last week. How do you perceive them being ideally manifested? What behaviors or activities represent each value for you? What should you do (or not do) to lead a life in accordance with each value?

_____

_____

_____

_____

_____

_____

_____

_____

_____

Consider your day-to-day life as it is right now; how do your core values manifest in your life? What do you do (or not do) to keep true to these values? Are there situations or circumstances that might make it challenging to hold true to these values?

_____

_____

_____

_____

_____

_____

_____

_____

_____

_____

_____

_____

_____

_____

_____

_____

How do you envision being truer to your core values would affect your life? Think of different aspects of your life, including relationships, health, emotional well-being, career, and so on.

_____

_____

_____

_____

_____

_____

_____

_____

_____

_____

_____

_____

_____

_____

_____

_____

_____

_____

_____

WEEK 18

"**There is no exercise better for the heart than reaching down and lifting people up.**"

—JOHN HOLMES

People value different things, and sometimes what seems to be valued in society may not match what you value. One common value held by many is compassion. How would you define compassion? What does it mean to you?

_____

_____

_____

_____

_____

_____

_____

_____

_____

_____

_____

_____

_____

Imagine a situation where fostering the value of compassion would benefit your life. Consider situations where it could make life more challenging.

_____

_____

_____

_____

_____

_____

_____

_____

_____

_____

_____

_____

_____

_____

_____

_____

_____

_____

_____

_____

Reflecting on the previous prompts, how much do you value compassion in your life? Would you like to strengthen the presence of compassion? Where does compassion fall in your ranking of values? Is it one of your core values?

_____

_____

_____

_____

_____

_____

_____

_____

_____

_____

_____

_____

_____

_____

_____

_____

_____

"Your core values provide the compass that keeps you moving in the right direction."

—SUSAN DAVID

In today's world, we are constantly measured by how much we can produce and are encouraged to pursue an increase in task completion. What is your own perspective on productivity as a personal value? Are there less favorable things you can identify about the value of productivity?

_____

_____

_____

_____

_____

_____

_____

_____

_____

_____

_____

_____

_____

Imagine a situation where being more productive would bene-fit your life. Consider situations where it could make life more challenging.

_____

_____

_____

_____

_____

_____

_____

_____

_____

_____

_____

_____

_____

_____

_____

_____

_____

_____

_____

Reflecting on the previous prompts, how much do you value productivity? Would you like to strengthen its presence in your life? If you had to prioritize your core values, where would you rank productivity, if at all?

_____

_____

_____

_____

_____

_____

_____

_____

_____

_____

_____

_____

_____

_____

_____

_____

_____

_____

WEEK 20

"Nothing is more noble, nothing more venerable, than loyalty."

—CICERO

Loyalty is a value many hold dear. We are loyal to our families, our cultures, nations, favorite sports teams, and so on. What are your expectations regarding and to what degree do you value loyalty from others and from yourself?

_____

_____

_____

_____

_____

_____

_____

_____

_____

_____

_____

_____

_____

Would a greater sense of loyalty to and/or from particular people or groups be beneficial in your life? In what ways? Can you identify how being loyal could lead to less favorable outcomes?

_____

_____

_____

_____

_____

_____

_____

_____

_____

_____

_____

_____

_____

_____

_____

_____

_____

_____

_____

Reflecting on the previous prompts, how much of a priority is loyalty to you? Would you like to strengthen its presence in your life? In your list of core values, where, if at all, does loyalty fall?

_____

_____

_____

_____

_____

_____

_____

_____

_____

_____

_____

_____

_____

_____

_____

_____

_____

_____

WEEK 21

"Be not afraid of growing slowly; be afraid only of standing still."

—CHINESE PROVERB

Your choice to do this self-discovery journal is evidence that self-growth is important to you. How do you define self-growth? Would you consider self-growth to be a value of yours?

_____

_____

_____

_____

_____

_____

_____

_____

_____

_____

_____

_____

_____

Would a greater value for self-growth be beneficial in your life? In what ways? Can you identify how valuing self-growth could lead to less favorable outcomes?

_____

_____

_____

_____

_____

_____

_____

_____

_____

_____

_____

_____

_____

_____

_____

_____

_____

_____

Where does self-growth fall in your core value rankings, if at all? Would you like to strengthen its presence?

_____

_____

_____

_____

_____

_____

_____

_____

_____

_____

_____

_____

_____

_____

_____

_____

_____

_____

_____

_____

WEEK 22

"Living with integrity means behaving in ways that are in harmony with your personal values."

—BARBARA DE ANGELIS

Reflect on your core values and the behaviors you believe are consistent with them. Can you imagine any barriers to following through with acting as you think would be the most compatible with your values?

_____

_____

_____

_____

_____

_____

_____

_____

_____

_____

_____

_____

_____

_____

Are there ways you can overcome these barriers? List anything that comes to mind and as many ways to overcome these barriers as possible.

_____

_____

_____

_____

_____

_____

_____

_____

_____

_____

_____

_____

_____

_____

_____

_____

_____

_____

_____

What beliefs or behaviors are you willing to commit to changing or continuing in order to ensure that you are living your life according to your stated values?

_____

_____

_____

_____

_____

_____

_____

_____

_____

_____

_____

_____

_____

_____

_____

_____

_____

_____

_____

"Leaders honor their core values, but they are flexible in how they execute them."

—COLIN POWELL

Think of the core values you have identified. Could they contradict one another? Or could different situations or areas of your life render one of them more important than the others? For instance, perhaps you need to lie and sacrifice the value of honesty in order to remain loyal to a friend. Try to envision those situations in detail.

_____

_____

_____

_____

_____

_____

_____

_____

_____

_____

_____

_____

_____

What would be the most difficult part for you about encountering a face-off between your values? How would you resolve such issues? Try to be specific.

_____

_____

_____

_____

_____

_____

_____

_____

_____

_____

_____

_____

_____

_____

_____

_____

_____

_____

Consider the conflicting values you identified in the previous prompts. Is there a way to be more flexible with the behavior required by your values? In other words, are there other ways to behave that still uphold these values while minimizing the conflict between them?

_____

_____

_____

_____

_____

_____

_____

_____

_____

_____

_____

_____

_____

_____

_____

_____

_____

"I have learned that as long as I hold fast to my beliefs and values, and follow my own moral compass, then the only expectations I need to live up to are my own."

—MICHELLE OBAMA

It is easier to commit to something when we can imagine its benefits. How do you think living in accordance with your values could improve your life?

_____

_____

_____

_____

_____

_____

_____

_____

_____

_____

_____

Are there people in your life who might be affected by you living according to your values? Who are they? In what ways would your change influence their lives, both positively and negatively?

_____

_____

_____

_____

_____

_____

_____

_____

_____

_____

_____

_____

_____

_____

_____

_____

_____

What kinds of benefits would motivate you to keep your behaviors and beliefs closely aligned with your values? Be as specific as possible.

_____

_____

_____

_____

_____

_____

_____

_____

_____

_____

_____

_____

_____

_____

_____

_____

_____

_____

_____

_____

"Good values are like a magnet—they attract good people."

—JOHN WOODEN

Consider how your social circle reflects your core values. Are there certain people who you would like to bring closer or others with whom you would like to create more distance because of values? Do your values influence your social circle? Should they?

_____

_____

_____

_____

_____

_____

_____

_____

_____

_____

_____

_____

Might there be new communities or groups you would like to be affiliated with in order to strengthen your core values? Think of the specific ways you can get connected to such groups, and also consider challenges.

_____

_____

_____

_____

_____

_____

_____

_____

_____

_____

_____

_____

_____

_____

_____

_____

_____

_____

_____

Imagine that some external force was preventing you from being able to follow and live by your values. How would that make you feel, and how would it affect your life and your sense of authenticity and belonging?

_____

_____

_____

_____

_____

_____

_____

_____

_____

_____

_____

_____

_____

_____

_____

_____

_____

_____

_____

"**Your core values are the deeply held beliefs that authentically describe your soul.**"

—JOHN C. MAXWELL

Imagine being a fly on the wall at your own funeral. Picture a close family member giving a eulogy. Does it feel authentic to who you are, the values you hold, and how you would like to be perceived? Are there any feelings of remorse for not following different values?

_____

_____

_____

_____

_____

_____

_____

_____

_____

_____

_____

_____

_____

Now consider hearing the eulogy of a different person, maybe a colleague, a friend from a different area of your life, or a hobby partner. Does this eulogy sound different from what you envisioned in the previous prompt? Try to compare and contrast the eulogies you imagine being given by people from different areas of your life.

_____

_____

_____

_____

_____

_____

_____

_____

_____

_____

_____

_____

_____

_____

_____

_____

_____

_____

Reflect on the core values you have identified throughout the past few months. Considering the first two prompts, how closely does it look like you have aligned yourself with these values so far in your life? Are there any additions or changes you would like to make to your list of core values?

_____

_____

_____

_____

_____

_____

_____

_____

_____

_____

_____

_____

_____

_____

_____

_____

_____

PART 3

Purpose

Purpose is a key to feeling more fulfilled in life. Remembering what you're working toward reflects your values, honors your true self, helps guide your decisions and actions, and is a way to cope with adversity and distress. At times, however, finding a purpose can be an extremely complex task. How do you know if you have found your true purpose before fully committing to it? And once you do commit, does that mean you shouldn't put energy in other endeavors? Is purpose something you choose or something that your life circumstances choose for you?

The next weeks' prompts ask you to be curious about what is meaningful to you in different areas of your life. You will explore your goals and motives to help you develop clarity on what is truly meaningful to you so you can determine your life's purpose(s). Keep in mind that life is in constant flux, and so are you; your purpose can be fine-tuned, adjusted, or even shifted completely as you move through life. The bottom line, however, is that although your purpose might evolve as you grow, it is important always to have that sense of purpose in your life.

"He who has a 'why' to live can bear almost any 'how.'"

—FRIEDRICH NIETZSCHE

What are the five ideas or goals that are most important to you in your life—things that you cannot imagine your life without?

_____

_____

_____

_____

_____

_____

_____

_____

_____

_____

_____

_____

_____

_____

_____

What is the most worthwhile activity that is a part of your regular, day-to-day life? What motivates that activity? Think of the things that bring a sense of joy, excitement, and fulfillment.

_____

_____

_____

_____

_____

_____

_____

_____

_____

_____

_____

_____

_____

_____

_____

_____

_____

_____

Whittle this list down to the one or two activities and/or goals that are most important to you. Can you get a sense of your life's purpose from looking at those?

_____

_____

_____

_____

_____

_____

_____

_____

_____

_____

_____

_____

_____

_____

_____

_____

_____

_____

"Life is never made unbearable by circumstances, but only by lack of meaning and
purpose."

—VIKTOR FRANKL

What are the five least important things in your life? What
compels you to spend time on those things?

_____

_____

_____

_____

_____

_____

_____

_____

_____

_____

_____

_____

_____

_____

How much of your time do you spend on the things that you deem to be important and how much time do you spend on the less important things? What do you think drives you to split your energy this way?

_____

_____

_____

_____

_____

_____

_____

_____

_____

_____

_____

_____

_____

_____

_____

_____

Would you like to change the ratio of the energy you dedicate to things that are important to you versus those that are not? Can you think of ways to change that ratio? Be specific.

_____

_____

_____

_____

_____

_____

_____

_____

_____

_____

_____

_____

_____

_____

_____

_____

_____

_____

_____

"Define your priorities, know your values and believe in your purpose. Only then can you effectively share yourself with others."

—LES BROWN

Now we are going to start breaking it down. What do you want most for and from your family? For example, would you want your family to have higher social status, or are close relationships with everyone more important to pursue? Would you want your family to be more affirming of you, or would you be interested in more time for yourself?

_____

_____

_____

_____

_____

_____

_____

_____

_____

_____

What concrete steps can you take to achieve these things for your family and for yourself? What could you reinforce in your current routine, what could you add to it, and what could you remove?

_____

_____

_____

_____

_____

_____

_____

_____

_____

_____

_____

_____

_____

_____

_____

_____

_____

How does your family contribute to your sense of life's purpose?

_____

_____

_____

_____

_____

_____

_____

_____

_____

_____

_____

_____

_____

_____

_____

_____

_____

WEEK 30

"True happiness . . . is not attained through self-gratification, but through fidelity to a worthy purpose."

—HELEN KELLER

Consider your friendships. Do you feel you take on a certain role among your friends, like the caretaker, leader, or maybe arbitrator? Do you take on different roles depending on the friend?

_____

_____

_____

_____

_____

_____

_____

_____

_____

_____

_____

_____

_____

When, if ever, do you feel that your friends hinder you in your life's purpose? How can you work around those challenges while being respectful of all that is good in those relationships?

_____

_____

_____

_____

_____

_____

_____

_____

_____

_____

_____

_____

_____

_____

_____

_____

_____

How do your closest friendships and interpersonal relationships bring you closer to your sense of purpose? Does friendship itself give you a sense of purpose?

_____

_____

_____

_____

_____

_____

_____

_____

_____

_____

_____

_____

_____

_____

_____

_____

_____

_____

_____

WEEK 31

"As you become more clear about who you really are, you'll be better able to decide what is best for you—the first time around."

—OPRAH WINFREY

We spend much of our time at our jobs. What are the three most important aspects of your job or career?

_____

_____

_____

_____

_____

_____

_____

_____

_____

_____

_____

_____

_____

_____

Do the important aspects of your job give you a sense of fulfill-
ment and purpose? Are there other more minor details of your
job that give you a sense of meaning?

_____

_____

_____

_____

_____

_____

_____

_____

_____

_____

_____

_____

_____

_____

_____

_____

_____

_____

_____

Try to identify ways you could enhance what gives you a sense of meaning in your job. How can you minimize the things that stand in your way to feeling more fulfilled in your job or career?

_____

_____

_____

_____

_____

_____

_____

_____

_____

_____

_____

_____

_____

_____

_____

_____

_____

_____

WEEK 32

"The person without a purpose is like a ship without a rudder."

—THOMAS CARLYLE

Think of your community. You may define community in terms of your neighborhood or city, identity or hobbies, or your family or groups you belong to. What are the three most important goals to you within the context of community affiliation? Some examples might be maintaining solidarity, promoting a mission, or living in accordance with its values.

_____

_____

_____

_____

_____

_____

_____

_____

_____

_____

_____

_____

In your life within that community, are you pursuing your goals? Is there a way you wish to be more involved?

_____

_____

_____

_____

_____

_____

_____

_____

_____

_____

_____

_____

_____

_____

_____

_____

_____

_____

In what ways does your community contribute to or help create your sense of purpose? If you have trouble thinking of ways, do you think you could promote a sense of purpose through finding a more relevant community?

_____

_____

_____

_____

_____

_____

_____

_____

_____

_____

_____

_____

_____

_____

_____

_____

"**People take different roads seeking fulfill-ment and happiness. Just because they're not on your road doesn't mean they've gotten lost.**"

—DALAI LAMA

Do you have spiritual beliefs? Do your beliefs ascribe a purpose to life? If so, do you agree with the stated or implied purpose?

_____

_____

_____

_____

_____

_____

_____

_____

_____

_____

_____

Take a closer look at your spiritual beliefs. Where or whom did these beliefs come from? Are they true to you? Or are they driven by the expectations of your community or family? Would you want to let go of any of these beliefs?

_____

_____

_____

_____

_____

_____

_____

_____

_____

_____

_____

_____

_____

_____

_____

_____

In what ways does your spiritual life help you? Does it align with your individual sense of your life's purpose?

_____

_____

_____

_____

_____

_____

_____

_____

_____

_____

_____

_____

_____

_____

_____

_____

_____

_____

_____

_____

WEEK 34

"Efforts and courage are not enough without purpose and direction."

—JOHN F. KENNEDY

Think of three to five things you believe in that are important to stand up for. Think of why you believe in these causes and what type of growth you would like to see in those areas. Be as specific as possible.

_____

_____

_____

_____

_____

_____

_____

_____

_____

_____

_____

_____

_____

_____

Looking at the previous prompt, are there ways you could be more involved in promoting these causes?

_____

_____

_____

_____

_____

_____

_____

_____

_____

_____

_____

_____

_____

_____

_____

_____

_____

_____

_____

_____

Imagine that you are able to be more engaged in the areas you identified as important. How do you believe it would affect your life? Do you see any downsides to being involved? Would it contribute to your sense of purpose?

_____

_____

_____

_____

_____

_____

_____

_____

_____

_____

_____

_____

_____

_____

_____

_____

_____

_____

"**Creativity is a great motivator because it makes people interested in what they are doing.**"

—EDWARD DE BONO

Creativity comes in many forms, but it is a driving force for all humans. Think about "being creative" as simply the act of creating something, whether or not it is artistic in a conventional sense. What do you create in your life? What do you create with your life? How do you feel when you are creating?

_____

_____

_____

_____

_____

_____

_____

_____

_____

_____

_____

_____

_____

Are there forms of creative work that you've always wanted to try but never have? What has gotten in the way? Be specific about the challenges and obstacles.

_____

_____

_____

_____

_____

_____

_____

_____

_____

_____

_____

_____

_____

_____

_____

_____

_____

_____

_____

Considering the previous two prompts, are there any new ways of being creative you can bring into your life now? Do you want to start cooking more? Making pottery? Organizing meet-ups? Learning how to complete projects around your house? Think about whether bringing those new ways into your life would give you a feeling of greater purpose.

_____

_____

_____

_____

_____

_____

_____

_____

_____

_____

_____

_____

_____

_____

_____

_____

_____

_____

WEEK 36

"Every great achiever is inspired by a mentor."

—LAILAH GIFTY AKITA

Imagine yourself as a contestant on the show *Jeopardy!*, where any topic can come up. What would you want your questions to be about? What is your area of expertise, the one you feel most comfortable with? Be specific in reasoning about your choice.

_____

_____

_____

_____

_____

_____

_____

_____

_____

_____

_____

_____

_____

_____

Consider your area of knowledge identified in the previous question. How would you feel if you could pass that knowledge and experience along to your child, a friend, or a stranger? Describe the thoughts and feelings going through your mind as you mentor someone on this topic.

_____

_____

_____

_____

_____

_____

_____

_____

_____

_____

_____

_____

_____

_____

_____

_____

_____

Do you believe being a mentor would add a sense of fulfillment to your life? Can you identify the ways you could enhance your sense of purpose by mentoring others? Be specific about how you could do that in your daily life.

"The meaning of life is to find your gift. The purpose of life is to give it away."

—DAVID VISCOTT

Imagine that you have an unlimited amount of money. What two or three causes would you like to contribute to and why? Do you feel like these causes resonate with your life's purpose?

_____

_____

_____

_____

_____

_____

_____

_____

_____

_____

_____

_____

_____

_____

Imagine that you didn't have to work for a salary. What would you dedicate your time to? List two or three activities you would prioritize. Do you feel like these align with your life's purpose?

_____

_____

_____

_____

_____

_____

_____

_____

_____

_____

_____

_____

_____

_____

_____

_____

_____

_____

Is the place you would put your time the same as the place you would put your money? Why or why not? Do any of these ideas stand out to you as feeling more in line with your life's purpose?

_____

_____

_____

_____

_____

_____

_____

_____

_____

_____

_____

_____

_____

_____

_____

_____

_____

_____

WEEK 38

"The purpose of life is a life of purpose."

—ROBERT BYRNE

Imagine that you have reached retirement, whatever that might look like for you. What are you most proud of having accomplished in your work life? This can be something you have actually already accomplished or something you plan to accomplish.

_____

_____

_____

_____

_____

_____

_____

_____

_____

_____

_____

_____

_____

_____

Now imagine watching a montage of photos of you throughout your whole life. What do they tell you? How do you feel about the display? Do the photos remind you of any special personal accomplishments you feel especially proud of?

_____

_____

_____

_____

_____

_____

_____

_____

_____

_____

_____

_____

_____

_____

_____

_____

_____

Reflecting on the previous two questions, where are you, if at all, on the path to your most purpose-filled life? If you're not in the place you would like to be, what needs to change, and what goals do you need to set?

_____

_____

_____

_____

_____

_____

_____

_____

_____

_____

_____

_____

_____

_____

_____

_____

_____

_____

_____

"It's not enough to have lived. We should be determined to live for something."

—WINSTON S. CHURCHILL

Where do you see yourself in 10 to 20 years? Where do you want to live, and who do you want close to you? What do you see being the most gratifying for your future self?

_____

_____

_____

_____

_____

_____

_____

_____

_____

_____

_____

_____

_____

_____

Continue reflecting on your future self and imagining your conversation with your future self. What would your future self describe as meaningful and important? Does your future self have any regrets in terms of finding meaning in life?

_____

_____

_____

_____

_____

_____

_____

_____

_____

_____

_____

_____

_____

_____

_____

_____

_____

Look back over the entries for the past 13 weeks, during which you've been writing about your purpose. Define what you have found to be your ultimate purpose(s) in life.

_____

_____

_____

_____

_____

_____

_____

_____

_____

_____

_____

_____

_____

_____

_____

_____

_____

_____

_____

_____

PART 4

Self-Love

Most people yearn to feel loved, cared for, and appreciated. We live and breathe by being liked in person and on social media, and we put forth a lot of effort to gain outside approval. What if you could put much of this energy into loving yourself and appreciating who you are? How might it feel to simply love yourself? Self-love is energizing, builds self-esteem, and provides us with fuel to grow.

During the next few months, you will work to uncover the aspects of yourself you struggle with, gaining insight into them and understanding what it is you do not love. You will attempt to accept your human limitations and imperfection and work with them rather than battle them. The objective is to subsume self-deprecation, self-loathing, and self-doubt as you discover ways to foster self-compassion, kindness, and self-love. Remember, no one will see this journal other than you, so be honest and allow yourself to express the thoughts and feelings you feel you can express to no one.

WEEK 40

"Accept yourself, love yourself, and keep moving forward. If you want to fly, you have to give up what weighs you down."

—ROY T. BENNETT

We all have some parts of ourselves that are challenging to accept. Identify three to five things about yourself that you tend to see in a negative light. Consider appearance, personality characteristics, beliefs, behaviors, and circumstances. Elaborate on what makes it difficult to accept each.

_____

_____

_____

_____

_____

_____

_____

_____

_____

_____

_____

_____

How do you react to the "faults" you described in the previous question? What is your self-talk? Are you self-punitive and critical? Do you believe you can change and grow, or do you believe you cannot control your ways?

_____

_____

_____

_____

_____

_____

_____

_____

_____

_____

_____

_____

_____

_____

_____

_____

_____

_____

Think of how you can develop a kinder, more loving approach toward the parts of you that you identified as difficult to love. Rather than seeing them as struggles, can you start to view them as challenges? What can you do or say to yourself that would promote self-compassion and growth?

_____

_____

_____

_____

_____

_____

_____

_____

_____

_____

_____

_____

_____

_____

_____

_____

_____

_____

WEEK 41

"Your task is not to seek for Love, but merely to seek and find all the barriers within yourself that you have built against it."

—HELEN SCHUCMAN

Think of your answers from last week. In what ways do you think not liking these parts of yourself may actually serve you? In what ways is resisting these parts of yourself protective, motivating, or helpful in your life? For example, maybe not liking your appearance prevents you from meeting new people, which in turn protects you from a potential rejection.

_____

_____

_____

_____

_____

_____

_____

_____

_____

_____

If your judgments about yourself disappeared, how would that influence your life? Be as specific as you can, thinking of all aspects of your life. Can you imagine there would be any negative results from eliminating your self-judgment?

_____

_____

_____

_____

_____

_____

_____

_____

_____

_____

_____

_____

_____

_____

_____

_____

_____

_____

Consider your answer to the previous prompts. Are there other ways to maintain the positive results of these self-judgments without the punitive or negative self-talk?

_____

_____

_____

_____

_____

_____

_____

_____

_____

_____

_____

_____

_____

_____

_____

_____

_____

_____

_____

WEEK 42

"Love yourself unconditionally, just as you love those closest to you despite their faults."

—LES BROWN

What is the one thing you find the hardest to love about yourself? How do you think that not loving this part of yourself affects your daily life and relationships? What feelings come up?

_____

_____

_____

_____

_____

_____

_____

_____

_____

_____

_____

_____

When you think about that single aspect of yourself, what is the judgment you are making? Who else do you imagine holds these judgments of you? And how does it feel to be judged that way?

_____

_____

_____

_____

_____

_____

_____

_____

_____

_____

_____

_____

_____

_____

_____

_____

_____

_____

_____

Imagine talking to someone you deeply care about. Suppose they confide in you that they, too, feel inadequate. Play out a dialogue between the two of you. Would you be supportive or critical of them? Can you envision responding to yourself the same way you respond to them?

_____

_____

_____

_____

_____

_____

_____

_____

_____

_____

_____

_____

_____

_____

_____

_____

_____

"Wanting to be someone else is a waste of the person you are."

—MARILYN MONROE

We all wish that we were more like someone or another, and we imagine that if we were only able to change one thing about ourselves, we would feel happier or complete. Think of the one thing that you imagine changing and how you believe it would lead to an improvement in your life. Try to uncover the underlying need, whether it be approval, belonging, settling anxiety, or something else entirely.

_____

_____

_____

_____

_____

_____

_____

_____

_____

_____

Imagine that you could magically switch places with another person. Who would you choose to switch with? What do you imagine would be the qualities you would gain from walking in that person's shoes? What do you imagine they would learn and gain from being you?

_____

_____

_____

_____

_____

_____

_____

_____

_____

_____

_____

_____

_____

_____

_____

_____

_____

Can you acknowledge aspects of yourself that are unique to who you are—desirable qualities that you may not be recognizing or dismissing as qualities?

_____

_____

_____

_____

_____

_____

_____

_____

_____

_____

_____

_____

_____

_____

_____

_____

_____

_____

_____

_____

WEEK 44

"One of the greatest regrets in life is being what others would want you to be, rather than being yourself."

—SHANNON L. ALDER

What were the messages about self-love you received while growing up? Was self-love a value that was emphasized and promoted in your family? Or was self-sacrifice a more dominant narrative? What is your perspective on people who practice self-love? Do you consider it to be empowering, self-indulgent, egotistical, or life-affirming?

_____

_____

_____

_____

_____

_____

_____

_____

_____

_____

_____

What beliefs hold you back from accepting and loving yourself fully? Are there other people's voices in your mind that challenge your self-love?

_____

_____

_____

_____

_____

_____

_____

_____

_____

_____

_____

_____

_____

_____

_____

_____

_____

_____

_____

_____

List all the reasons why it would be challenging to overcome these barriers to self-love. Are you willing to put in the work to overcome the barriers? Think of some specific barriers and steps you can take to challenge them.

_____

_____

_____

_____

_____

_____

_____

_____

_____

_____

_____

_____

_____

_____

_____

_____

_____

_____

_____

WEEK 45

"Why should we worry about what others think of us, do we have more confidence in their opinions than we do our own?"

—BRIGHAM YOUNG

Think about some of your self-limiting beliefs: the voices that tell you that you are not good enough or not worthy enough or that you cannot be loved until you achieve a certain goal, look, or status. Where did you first get that message? How did you learn that about yourself?

_____

_____

_____

_____

_____

_____

_____

_____

_____

_____

_____

_____

_____

Can you detect the ways you reinforce those self-limiting beliefs in your daily life? In your self-talk? In your conversations with others? In preventing yourself from trying certain things? Do you trust your own voice or the voices of other people when it comes to opinions about yourself?

_____

_____

_____

_____

_____

_____

_____

_____

_____

_____

_____

_____

_____

_____

_____

_____

_____

_____

Identify some ways you invalidate or dismiss your own opinions and feelings for those of others. Are there situations where you do that more? How can you reinforce the trust in your own ideas about yourself?

_____

_____

_____

_____

_____

_____

_____

_____

_____

_____

_____

_____

_____

_____

_____

_____

_____

_____

_____

WEEK 46

"A man cannot be comfortable without his own approval."

—MARK TWAIN

Moving past other people's judgments is very challenging, but getting past our own judgments can feel impossible at times. Can you identify the three most common judgments you have about yourself? For example, you may have in your head that you are a terrible athlete, you can't do math, and you aren't good at socializing at large parties.

_____

_____

_____

_____

_____

_____

_____

_____

_____

_____

_____

Think of each judgment identified in the previous question. What feelings does each bring up for you? What are the most common feelings you feel about yourself given those judgments?

_____

_____

_____

_____

_____

_____

_____

_____

_____

_____

_____

_____

_____

_____

_____

_____

_____

_____

_____

_____

In what ways could you cultivate self-compassion, acceptance, and self-love toward your human limitations and their impact on you?

_____

_____

_____

_____

_____

_____

_____

_____

_____

_____

_____

_____

_____

_____

_____

_____

_____

_____

WEEK 47

"Owning our story and loving ourselves through that process is the bravest thing that we'll ever do."

—BRENÉ BROWN

We each have our own story about who we are, and we tend to find it difficult to readjust. We defend our perceptions of ourselves, even if they do not necessarily match who we are in the present. Reflect on your own narrative. What are some aspects of yourself that still match your current sense of self? Are there other aspects that no longer reflect who you are these days?

_____

_____

_____

_____

_____

_____

_____

_____

_____

_____

Consider the aspects of yourself you are trying to hold on to. Do these aspects of yourself contribute to self-love or prevent it? What would it mean to your life if you let them go?

_____

_____

_____

_____

_____

_____

_____

_____

_____

_____

_____

_____

_____

_____

_____

_____

_____

_____

_____

Rewrite your narrative, incorporating some new perspectives into the existing one to promote self-love.

_____

_____

_____

_____

_____

_____

_____

_____

_____

_____

_____

_____

_____

_____

_____

_____

_____

_____

_____

_____

_____

WEEK 48

"When we are mindful, deeply in touch with the present moment, our understanding of what is going on deepens, and we begin to be filled with acceptance, joy, peace and love."

—THICH NHAT HANH

Mindfulness is the act of being fully present and engaged in the moment without assigning any positive or negative judgments about it. Reflect on how much of your day you are able to be present mindfully and how often your mind goes to judgments, regrets of the past, or fears for the future. Describe the moment you are truly mindful.

_____

_____

_____

_____

_____

_____

_____

_____

_____

_____

Are there situations, places, or people with whom you find it more challenging to be in the moment and practice mindfulness? Are there certain thoughts or emotions you carry that make it more difficult to stay present in the moment? Are there times in your day when you find it easier to focus on the present moment? Be specific.

Being mindful enhances your self-love, which in turn gives you the energy you need to continue your existence, growth, and prosperity. Take the time to write down a concrete plan to practice mindfulness. Be as specific as you can in making your plan, with days, times, and circumstances in which you will tune in and be mindful.

_____

_____

_____

_____

_____

_____

_____

_____

_____

_____

_____

_____

_____

_____

_____

_____

_____

_____

"When you recover or discover something that nourishes your soul and brings joy, care enough about yourself to make room for it in your life."

—JEAN SHINODA BOLEN

How do you personally define joy and happiness? What do they look like for you in practice?

_____

_____

_____

_____

_____

_____

_____

_____

_____

_____

_____

_____

_____

_____

_____

You cannot have joy if you do not love yourself, and although loving yourself does not promise joy, it is an essential component and a great step toward it. Think of all the things that instill a sense of joy in your life. Which of them also promote your sense of self-love?

_____

_____

_____

_____

_____

_____

_____

_____

_____

_____

_____

_____

_____

_____

In what ways can you engage in more experiences that promote self-love and joy? Be as specific as possible.

_____

_____

_____

_____

_____

_____

_____

_____

_____

_____

_____

_____

_____

_____

_____

_____

_____

_____

_____

WEEK 50

"Love yourself enough to set boundaries. Your time and energy are precious. You get to choose how you use it. You teach people how to treat you by deciding what you will and won't accept."

—ANNA TAYLOR

What are your expectations about how you should be treated by your family, your friends, your partner, and yourself?

_____

_____

_____

_____

_____

_____

_____

_____

_____

_____

_____

_____

To what extent do you feel like those expectations are being met or unmet? Think of all aspects of your life and be specific.

_____

_____

_____

_____

_____

_____

_____

_____

_____

_____

_____

_____

_____

_____

_____

_____

_____

_____

_____

How you are being treated by others, and certainly by yourself, affects your underlying ability to love yourself. In what ways can you ask for what you need or make your needs clearer if they are not being met? Can you make a list of nonnegotiables?

_____

_____

_____

_____

_____

_____

_____

_____

_____

_____

_____

_____

_____

_____

_____

_____

_____

"When you make a mistake, respond to yourself in a loving way rather than a self-shaming way."

—ELLIE HOLCOMB

Think of what you consider to be a mistake you've made. How did you react to it, in your actions and internally? What thoughts, feelings, and urges did you experience?

_____

_____

_____

_____

_____

_____

_____

_____

_____

_____

_____

_____

_____

Consider your past experiences. How did other people respond
to you when you made a mistake as a child and later on in
your life? Did you internalize these reactions?

_____

_____

_____

_____

_____

_____

_____

_____

_____

_____

_____

_____

_____

_____

_____

_____

_____

_____

_____

_____

Create a mantra you can incorporate into your regular thinking to mediate any negative internal reaction to making mistakes. Make sure it has a loving tone rather than a harsh one. For instance, repeat to yourself: "Everyone makes mistakes; it is human and how we learn and grow."

_____

_____

_____

_____

_____

_____

_____

_____

_____

_____

_____

_____

_____

_____

_____

_____

_____

WEEK 52

"The real difficulty is to overcome how you think about yourself."

—MAYA ANGELOU

Abundance mentalities is the mindset of having endless opportunities for change, growth, and success. Scarcity mentality is the belief that your options are limited, leading to a fear of never being able to have your needs met. Where do you believe you fall on the continuum between those two mentalities? In what ways can you imagine that your mentality affects your life?

_____

_____

_____

_____

_____

_____

_____

_____

_____

_____

Similarly, mentality of abundance of love and scarcity of love can influence your emotions and ability to perceive and receive love from others and yourself. Reflect on your own concept of love and self-love. Are there circumstances when you feel that you are unable to love yourself? How does it feel physically and emotionally to experience love? Exciting, frightening, or maybe both? How can you allow more love in? How can you add more self-love practices to your routine?

_____

_____

_____

_____

_____

_____

_____

_____

_____

_____

_____

_____

_____

_____

_____

_____

Write down a specific list, which you can keep and refer to when you need it, of all of the times that self-love comes easily to you. Or write a "love letter" to yourself containing all the aspects of you that you love.

_____

_____

_____

_____

_____

_____

_____

_____

_____

_____

_____

_____

_____

_____

_____

_____

_____

_____

_____

_____

Parting Words

Be proud of yourself! A year ago, you decided to start a journey of self-discovery, and now you have completed this one major piece. During the past 52 weeks, you have bravely stood in front of a mirror and taken a really intense look, acknowledged your truth, where you stand, and where you would like to be in terms of self-awareness, values, purpose, and self-love. Whether this was your first step on your road to self-discovery or you have been practicing self-exploration for many years, I hope that this journey allowed you to deepen your connection to yourself and your loved ones.

Over the next few weeks, try to look back at your answers from the past year. Consider taking the time to allow the insights you have gained to be assimilated into your way of thinking, acting, and being. You can also consider which areas would be important for you to focus on as you continue to grow.

Go back and look at this journal whenever you feel you want to refocus on who you truly are. Remember always to be open, flexible, accepting of change as time goes by, and, most importantly, kind to yourself.

Resources

Additional Reading

Self-awareness: *The Four Agreements: A Practical Guide to Personal Freedom* by Don Miguel Ruiz

Values: *The Book of Joy: Lasting Happiness in a Changing World* by Dalai Lama, Desmond Tutu, and Douglas Carlton Abrams

Purpose: *The Café on the Edge of the World: A Story about the Meaning of Life* by John Strelecky

Self-love: *The Mastery of Love: A Practical Guide to the Art of Relationship* by Don Miguel Ruiz

Free Mindfulness Resources

Chopra Center Meditation: ChopraCenterMeditation.com
UCLA Mindful Awareness Research Center: UCLAHealth.org/marc/mindful-meditations
Tara Brach Guided Meditations: TaraBrach.com/guided-meditations

References

"20 Famous and Wise Chinese Proverbs (谚语 Yanyu), Say-
ings and Quotes: Chinese, Pinyin, English Translation
and Standing Still - Jewel (Lyrics) - Chinesetolearn 🎵
Learn Mandarin in a Fun Way 🎵." Chinesetolearn, February 19, 2015. http://www.chinesetolearn.com/20-famou
s-and-wise-chinese-proverbs-%E8%B0%9A%E8%AF%AD-yan
yu-sayings-and-quotes/.

Abdelnour, Ziad K. "Ziad K Abdelnour Quotes: Ziad K Abdelnour."
Ziad K Abdelnour. Accessed May 24, 2021. https://www.ziadkab-
delnour.com/ziad-k-abdelnour-quotes/.

Akita, Lailah Gifty. Think Great, Be Great! New York, NY: Createspace, 2014.

Allan, David. "A Life of Purpose Brings Meaning to a Senseless
Death." BBC Worklife. BBC. Accessed May 24, 2021. https://www.
bbc.com/worklife/article/20140827-a-life-and-death-with-purpose.

Angelou, Maya, and Arthur Austen Douglas. 928 Maya Angelou
Quotes. CreateSpace Independent Publishing Platform, 2016.

Bach, Richard, and Russell Munson. Jonathan Livingston Seagull: a
Story. London: HarperThorsons, 2015.

Bennett, Roy T. The Light in the Heart: Inspirational Thoughts for
Living Your Best Life. United States: Roy T. Bennett, 2020.

Bolen, Jean Shinoda. Like a Tree: How Trees, Women, and
Tree People Can Save the Planet. Newburyport: Red Wheel
Weiser, 2011.

Brown Brené. Braving the Wilderness: the Quest for True Belonging and the Courage to Stand Alone. New York, NY: Random House, 2019.

Brown, Les. It's Not over until You Win!: How to Become the Person You Always Wanted to Be, No Matter What the Obstacle. New York, NY: Simon & Schuster, 1998.

Brown, Les. Live Your Dreams. New York: Quill, 2001.

Carlyle, Thomas. The Complete Works of Thomas Carlyle. New York, NY: Thomas Y. Crowell & Co, 1902.

Chidac, Daniel. Who Says You Can't? You Do. Harmony, 2013.

Churchill, Winston, and Michael Wolff. The Collected Essays of Sir Winston Churchill. London (44 Museum St., WC1A 1LY), UK: Library of Imperial History, 1976.

Cicero, Marcus Tullius, and Cyrus R. Edmonds. Cicero's Three Books of Offices, or Moral Duties; Also His Cato Major ... Laelius ... Paradoxes; Scipio's Dream; and Letter to Quintus on the Duties of a Magistrate. Literally Tr., with Notes .. New York: Harper & Bros., 1857.

Company, The John Maxwell. "The Law of Awareness: 4 Questions to Help You Know Yourself." John Maxwell, April 8, 2013. https://www.johnmaxwell.com/blog/the-law-of-awareness-4-questions-to-help-you-know-yourself/.

David, Susan A. Emotional Agility: Get Unstuck, Embrace Change, and Thrive in Work and Life. Great Britain: Penguin Life, 2017.

De Bono, Edward. Lateral Thinking: Creativity Step by Step. New York, NY: Harper & Row, 1970.

Downs, Robyn Conley, and Briana Summers. The Feel Good Effect: Reclaim Your Wellness by Finding Small Shifts That Create Big Change. Emeryville, CA: Ten Speed Press, 2020.

Ford, Debbie. "Consciousness Cleanse Day 2: The Gift of Self-Awareness." Oprah.com. Oprah.com, January 5, 2010. https://www.oprah.com/spirit/consciousness-cleanse-day-2-the-gift-of-self-awareness.

Frankl, Viktor E. Man's Search for Ultimate Meaning. London: Rider, 2011.

Frankl, Victor. Man's Search for Meaning. London: Rider Books, 2020.

Harari, Oren. The Leadership Secrets of Colin Powell. New York, NY: McGraw-Hill, 2003.

Holcomb, Ellie. "Fighting Words Friday: Do Everything In Love." Ellie Holcomb. Ellie Holcomb, January 9, 2020. https://www.ellieholcomb.com/blog-2/2019/1/11/fighting-words-friday-do-everything-in-love.

Jagyasi, Dr Prem. "Your Values Are Embedded within You Irrespective of Whether You Discover." Dr Prem Jagyasi's Quotes, October 10, 2020. https://drprem.com/quotes/your-values-are-embedded-within-you-irrespective-of-whether-you-discover-them-or-not-even-if-you-never-find-them-they-still-govern-your-life/.

Jung, C. G. Selected Letters of C.g. Jung, 1909-1961. Princeton, NJ: Princeton University Press, 2016.

Keller, Helen. The Open Door. Berkeley, CA: University of California, 1957.

Kennedy, John F. "Speech of Senator John F. Kennedy, Raleigh, NC, Coliseum." Speech of Senator John F. Kennedy, Raleigh, NC, Coliseum | The American Presidency Project, September 17, 1960. https://www.presidency.ucsb.edu/documents/speech-senator-john-f-kennedy-raleigh-nc-coliseum.

Kirsten, Max. Self-Help: Find Your Self to Help Yourself. Carlsbad: Hay House, Inc., 2011.

Liu, Charles. "Mandarin Monday: Learn Inspirational Chinese Proverbs Both Real and Fake." the Beijinger. the beijinger, March 13, 2017. https://www.thebeijinger.com/blog/2017/03/13/mandarin-monday-inspirational-chinese-proverbs.

MAKERS, THE SUCCESS. I LOVE MYSELF: over 1,700 Words of Wisdom to Inspire You to Achieve Greatness in Your Life. LULU COM, 2017.

Maxwell, John C. The 5 Levels of Leadership: Proven Steps to Maximise Your Potential. New York, NY: Center Street, 2013.

McLeod, Melvin, and Thich Nhat Hanh. Your True Home. Boulder, CO: Shambhala, 2011.

Newmark, Amy. Chicken Soup for the Soul: the Power of Yes!: 101 Stories about Adventure, Change and Positive Thinking. Cos Cob, CT: Chicken Soup for the Soul, LLC, 2018.

Obama, Michelle. "Remarks by the First Lady at Tuskegee University Commencement Address." National Archives and Records Administration. National Archives and Records Administration, May 9, 2015. https://obamawhitehouse.archives.gov/the-press-office/2015/05/09/remarks-first-lady-tuskegee-university-commencement-address.

Osho. Learning to Silence the Mind: Wellness through Meditation. New York: St. Martin's Griffin, 2012.

Parton, Dolly. "Find out Who You Are and Do It on Purpose. #Dollyism Pic.twitter.com/3s4eiaGv6D." Twitter. Twitter, April 8, 2015. https://twitter.com/DollyParton/status/585890099583397888.

Ruiz, Miguel, and Nicholas Wilton. The Four Agreements: a Practical Guide to Personal Freedom. San Rafael, CA: Amber-Allen, 2012.

Schucman, Helen. A Course in Miracles. Tiburon, CA: Foundation for Inner Peace, 1985.

Smith, Rich. "Values Are like Fingerprints." Atlas Med-Staff. Accessed May 24, 2021. https://atlasmedstaff.com/adventures-in-nursing/values-are-like-fingerprints/.

"Top 50 Buddhist Quotes." ReflectandRespond, February 21, 2021. https://reflectandrespond.com/top-50-buddhist-quotes/.

Toren, Adam. "5 Quotes to Help You Conquer Your Fears." Entrepreneur, October 30, 2014. https://www.entrepreneur.com/article/238698.

Twain, Mark. What Is Man? and Other Essays of Mark Twain. South Bend, IN: Infomotions, Inc., 2001.

Viscott, David. Finding Your Strength in Difficult Times: a Book of Meditations. New York, NY: McGraw-Hill, 2003.

Winfrey, Oprah, and Bill Adler. The Uncommon Wisdom of Oprah Winfrey: a Portrait in Her Own Words. London, UK: Aurum, 1997.

Wolfelt, Alan. Grief One Day at a Time: 365 Meditations to Help You Heal after Loss. Fort Collins, CO: Companion Press, 2016.

Wooden, John R., and Steve Jamison. Wooden on Leadership. New York, NY: McGraw-Hill, 2005.

Frankl, Victor. Man's Search for Meaning. London: Rider Books, 2020.

About the Author

 **Yana Lechtman**, PsyD, is a licensed clinical psychologist. She graduated from Ferkauf Graduate School of Psychology at Yeshiva University and completed her postdoctoral fellowship at Lenox Hill Hospital in New York City. Her work has been presented at American Academy of Child and Adolescent Psychiatry and Association for Behavioral and Cognitive Therapies (AACAP and ABCT) conferences, and she has contributed to several published articles. She has worked with children, adults, and families in various settings, including acute inpatient units, intensive day treatment programs, and outpatient, residential, and in-home settings.

Dr. Lechtman specializes in working with people who experience emotional dysregulation, difficulties in relationships, and challenges related to identity development and transitions. She is also experienced in working with those who struggle with suicidal thoughts and self-harm behaviors. She emphasizes the ability to be curious and playful in the process of self-exploration, believes in the importance of being kind and self-compassionate while developing ways to tolerate and navigate any emotional experience, and values the importance interpersonal connectedness and relationships.

1 eyelashes

2 white board pens or chalk board

3 car battery

4 Matches

5 potting soil

9 781648 767678